John Sanders' Lichfield

Words and wood engravings by himself

To Maisie

ISBN 1 899596 04 6

Abbotsford Publishing, 2a Brownsfield Road, Lichfield, Staffordshire WS13 6BT
October 1998

Printed by J. M. Tatler & Son Ltd, Abbey Street Works, Derby

Contents

BEEHIVE

FOREWORD

THE author of this work came to Lichfield in 1958 to be Principal of the School of Art. Although born and bred in Derbyshire, like many newcomers before him he rapidly developed an abiding affection for this ancient city, an affection that has lasted to this day.

Generations of students at the Art School will remember the events he organised in the city and especially the annual "Fiestas", the two great pageants of 1972 and 75, and the part he played in setting up the Arts Association under the sign of the "Red Umbrella". For all these achievements he was awarded a well-deserved MBE.

During the forty years he has lived in Lichfield, John Sanders has practised the art of wood engraving, and from a wonderful collection of subjects we have selected a number of particular interest to those who know and love the "Mother of the Midlands". These have been furnished with a commentary which all of those readers who know him will recognise immediately as typical of John; pithy, pertinent and full of the observant eye of the artist.

As a citizen of Lichfield, John has played a prominent part in the Society of Artists, the Civic Society, the Worshipful Company of Smiths and most of all in the Darwin Walk Trust of which he was the founder, and a founder member of the Erasmus Darwin Foundation. In spite of what he says about councillors, he has served as an elected member of Lichfield District Council. Truly he writes from personal experience!

Abbotsford Publishing are pleased to present this work to the public as a worthy addition to the bibliography of this city.

CATHEDRAL

SOME LICHFIELD BUILDINGS

LICHFIELD Cathedral, built over eight hundred years ago, is still, despite the introduction of new building techniques and new materials, the finest building within a radius of some thirty miles, and one of the biggest, only exceeded by out of town shopping centres, multi-storey car parks and colleges of higher technology (now called Universities).

It has been a joy to the beholder ever since it was built. Nevertheless, despite their deep religious affiliations, both sides in England's first and up to now, only Civil War, misused it in many disagreeable ways. But it still remained an inspiration. Those participants had bombarded it, mined it, used it as a fortress and stabled their horses in it. They left it, after victory, a dilapidated ruin without its central spire and with very inadequate accommodation for worshippers, or for that matter the men of the cloth.

It was rebuilt in the same century by Bishop Hacket and has been refurbished from time to time ever since. Now, however, thanks this time to European money and an entrepreneurial Dean and Chapter it is, but for the grime, very much as it would have appeared when it was new.

Its influence has at no time been greater, and numerous local businesses and organisations are named after it. We have the Three Spires Shopping Centre, The Three Spires Jazz Club, The Three Spires Photographic Club and The Three Golden Spires public house, no less. But why, I wonder, don't we have the Three Steeples something or other? And for that matter why isn't the Grand National a Spire Chase, or the chap repairing the weathercock, a Spire Jack?

Perhaps the next most noticeable building in the city is St. John's Hospital without the Barrs, with its eight tall and distinguished domestic chimneys, some of the oldest in the country. If you go through the Tudor archway where a notice says "No right of Way" you will find yourself in another world, Barchester Towers in fact. It is difficult to believe that all the motor traffic to and from most of our neighbouring towns, as well as the railway to Birmingham, goes past its walls. I think St. John Street should be made a one way street and halved in width. We would then have a chance to see its charm, but who am I to pontificate?

St. John's was once a refuge for travellers who needed protection from the brigands of Hopwas forest when they arrived at the city gate (the Barrs) after closing time. Safely, they rested in it until next morning when the gates opened and they could enter the city to face the other brigands therein.

It now houses elderly gentlemen and protects them from the End of Millennium rat race.

Milley's Hospital, also dating from Tudor times, does the same for the ladies. Recently both have been considerably enlarged and now lucky married pensioners are actually allowed to live together in a new development.

ST. JOHN'S HOSPITAL WITHOUT THE BARRS

MILLEY'S HOSPITAL FOR ELDERLY LADIES

Saint Chad's must be the oldest parish church in Lichfield. In fact, since the saint himself settled nearby on first coming down from Northumberland to convert the local heathens, it must be the oldest Christian site in the Midlands. Little, if anything of the original building exists today, maybe a few bits of stone. But the well in the churchyard still holds water and from that watery pulpit the saint is said to have preached the gospel. Uncomfortable for him, no doubt, but memorable showmanship.

The present church is mostly mediaeval with a seventeenth century clerestory. It stands in one of the most attractive positions in the city and the road to Stafford used to run past its western walls.

The most recent of our Anglican parish churches is Christ Church which was built by Mrs. Hinckley, formerly Mrs. Robinson, and the mother of the two little girls whose memorial, by Sir Francis Chantrey, is perhaps the best known monument in the cathedral. She built Christ Church as a memorial to all the many close members of her family who had left this world. This was in the first half of the nineteenth century and soon after its finish the churchyard was to become the last resting place of her only son. Her life was full of tragedy.

Overleaf can be seen the house in which Dr. Erasmus Darwin lived whilst he practised as Lichfield's most successful physician in the eighteenth century. It had been practically rebuilt on the Jacobean foundations of what must have been a very substantial dwelling but the alterations made it one of the most elegant houses in the city.

St. Chad's Church

Christ Church

However, it has throughout the years been very much neglected, until just a few years ago when a group of Darwin enthusiasts and the owners, the Dean and Chapter, got together and decided to do something about it. Now, thanks to these enthusiasts, Europe and the Lottery, things are changing and by the time this book goes to press the house should be once more refurbished and operating as a centre for the study of things related to the doctor and his work and their relationship to Christianity.

The other picture is of Streethay Wharf, now Streethay Marina. Erasmus Darwin and his friends, Josiah Wedgwood and James Brindley had hoped to bring a canal into the city, to a wharf, in fact, at Minster pool. This scheme came to nothing but another canal came as close to the town as Shortbutts Lane (Gallows Wharf) and its dried up course is easily identifiable on that stretch behind the lane which is now part of the Darwin Walk.

This canal could well be re-established in the near future.

DARWIN'S HOUSE

LICHFIELD DOCKLAND, STREETHAY

PEOPLE

OVER the centuries, many people of note have lived in Lichfield, but most particularly in the eighteenth century. Of these Sam Johnson is undoubtedly the best known, and in the following pages can be seen his birthplace at the corner of Market Street and Breadmarket Street and the man himself enjoying a pot of tea, (the beverage which gave him so much pleasure) and overleaf with his friend and one time pupil David Garrick, setting off for London, fame and fortune with a single horse between them, all they could afford.

They took it in turns to ride in a sort of leapfrogging pattern. The first rider, leaving at a trot, tied up his mount at a suitable point further along the road and continued on foot. He was overtaken in due course by his travelling companion, after that individual had reached Dobbin, mounted, and covered *his* few miles in the luxury of a saddle and so on until, after one hundred and twenty miles, they reached the "Great Wen."

They both did quite well in London. Johnson wrote a dictionary and said something rather significant about almost everything known at the time. And Garrick is still regarded as one of the greatest actors of all time despite the fact that it's two hundred years since anyone saw him perform.

Elias Ashmole and Joseph Addison lived in Lichfield before them, as did Sir John Floyer, a medical man who was the first practitioner to understand the importance of the pulse (after experiments on the inmates of St. John's and Milley's Hospitals) and Anna Seward, a century later, and known in her day as the Swan of Lichfield for her now somewhat discredited poetry. Nevertheless in its time it considerably impressed Sir Walter Scott. Come to that, what other woman poet of that early period is remembered at all?

Erasmus Darwin practised as a doctor in the city for twenty-five years and in the world of science his name will be remembered as long as will that of Samuel Johnson in the world of letters, and it must not be forgotten that Erasmus wrote many thousands of lines of verse in his numerous books on matters of science, verse not highly regarded today but thought of as top of the range in his day. At one time in that most entertaining period of Lichfield's history the young Anna Seward seems to have been somewhat in love with the widowed Erasmus, but his interests were directed elsewhere, in neighbouring Derbyshire. But that is another story.

JOHNSON'S BIRTHPLACE TODAY

HIMSELF

THE BOOK SHOP

9

SAM AND DAVIE SET OFF FOR LONDON

ERASMUS DISCOVERS ANNA'S
HEART CONDITION

Having dealt with those impressive and well remembered eighteenth century figures, I wonder how many others there have been who were very important in their day but are now languishing in obscurity?

The important and distinguished nineteenth century Chancellor Law is now largely remembered for his grandiose tomb in St. Michael's churchyard. It boasted a clock which was originally illuminated by the then new-fangled gas light and was designed by the Chancellor himself.

And on Greenhill there is also a memorial which is a gesture to the welfare of the many horses and ponies which then kept the transport system alive. It is a stone-built horse and cattle trough dedicated to the memory of (in case you've forgotten) the Rev. J. J. Sergeantson, M.A., rector of St. Michael's until 1886. He would, I feel sure, shed salty tears if he could see his memorial drinking facility now without water and with rather pathetic and almost indecipherable biblical texts sketchily extolling the virtues of this most valuable element once also drunk by humans. And our transport system now drinks fossil fuel!

Refuelling 19thC.

11

We had politicians and soldiers too, the Dyotts, the Ansons and Henry Paget, who was created Marquess of Anglesey for his leadership of Wellington's cavalry at Waterloo, but who later distinguished himself in politics and became a far sighted and enlightened Lord Lieutenant of Ireland for many troublesome years. Things appear to have been little better in the Emerald Isle in those days than they have been in more recent years.

Probably the best known Dyott was disabled and dubbed, because of his disability, Dumb Dyott; he gained fame during the Civil War by killing one of his fellow countrymen in Dam Street. This was Lord Brooke who happened to have found himself a political opponent.

And somewhat surprisingly, given Lichfield's Midland location, there have been mariners as well. The Earl of Lichfield inherits his title from his ancestor George Anson, who was a very successful naval commander and to whom the title was awarded after his circumnavigation of the world under sail, which, apart from rowing, was the only way to do it in those days; and nobody did that sort of thing just for fun!

Back on *terra firma* we must not forget the trumpeter, John Brown, who was buried in St. Michael's churchyard and is supposed to have sounded the Charge at the Battle of Balaclava, which sent so many brave men and conscripted horses — frightened men and terrified horses — to their deaths before the firing squad of enemy cannon and who today are immortalised in Tennyson's "Charge of the Light Brigade".

I don't think his spectre haunts any part of the city but there are supposed to be several others that do. There's a troop of civil war infantry that marches along Gaia Lane, and if you go into one of the houses in Breadmarket Street you might well be pulled out of bed by a well meaning ghost attempting to rescue you from a devastating fire that once caused death and destruction in that building.

Most important of all our spirits, however, is the spirit of Hector Beane. He was once the Master of the Guild of St. Mary and St. John (forerunner of the Mayor) and arranged for piped water to be available in Lichfield long before it became a feature of most larger towns. Perhaps, more importantly, he established the Conduit Lands charity which has been the major source of cash flow hereabouts ever since. Conduit Lands capital can be detected in the foundations of practically every worthwhile exercise the city has seen.

TRUMPETER JOHN BROWN

THE GHOST OF HECTOR BEANE

OTHER LICHFIELD PEOPLE

THERE have been other people of note over the years but none of them are likely to achieve the stature of the formidable Doctor Johnson and today we all seem rather alike and rather ordinary.

We have, in Lichfield, ordinary insurance brokers, ordinary teachers and policemen, ordinary stockbrokers and ordinary house breakers. The ordinary stockbroker may be able to afford Armani suits but he rarely wears one. He looks very much like his ordinary fellow citizens. Despite that, we all now seem to live more and more in semi-watertight compartments, mixing only with others of similar backgrounds and similar income.

The stockbroker who travels daily along the contaminated roads into Birmingham has no idea how the elderly teacher, who travels daily along the contaminated roads into Tamworth, confronts a stroppy, unco-operative schoolgirl; and the regular cathedral go-er knows hardly anything at all about what goes on, on a Saturday night in the local pubs. Worst of all, hardly anyone knows what their own local councillor looks like, unless he or she happens to be the much photographed Mayor or Sheriff. They don't care much either, as long as those incumbents don't allow anything undesirable to disrupt the placidity of their own particular neighbourhood.

There was a time when you could tell a postman by his uniform, the man who dug holes in the pavement by his inevitable little garters just below the knee, the shoeing smith by his divided apron and the solicitor, or the doctor, by his black jacket and striped trousers, and some occupations even demanded the wearing of a skirt; now it's all jeans.

When I came to Lichfield in 1958, I was told that the city was famous for its three P's: Parsons, Pubs and Prostitutes. It was easy to pick out the parsons, they all wore black and a few even wore breeches and gaiters, and as they walked about the city they produced a punctuating effect amongst all the grey, fawn and beige apparel worn by mere mortals. Now they wear anoraks, tee-shirts and bomber jackets in all colours like the rest of us. On the other hand secondary school pupils, who once wore distinctive uniforms which varied from navy blue to the Friary's splendid scarlet, now all wear black and the girls uniform skirts could well be described as longish cassocks or widish belts.

14

Externally, the pubs haven't changed much but some of the more ancient ones have been modernised inside by being made to look more Olde Worlde. This is achieved by having the original timbers replaced by plastic imitations.

I don't know what the prostitutes looked like either, then or now, though I understand there are now fewer of them. Maybe, however, like the men of the cloth, they are less easy to recognise!

THE WHEELS OF COMMERCE

GENERATION GAP

IN THE BLACK

CONTINUING PEOPLE

FUNNY thing about men of the cloth, they are all to some degree reverend, according to their particular job. We have the ordinary reverend, the very reverend, the right reverend and the most reverend. There are also a few nearly reverends and para-reverends. It happens in other spheres as well. When a peer dies, his, up to then, *honourable* son, becomes *noble*, a duke's son on his father's death becomes *graceful* and when his mother dies Prince Charles will become *Majestic*.

Dark skins are not commonplace in Lichfield but very few of our citizens were born here and in post war years there is a surprising number of foreign sounding names. I wonder when we will have a mayor with a name ending in *ski* or *stein*. Up to now I don't think we've even had a *Mac* or an *O'* at the beginning. However, like the rest of Britain, we have absorbed many features of foreign cultures. We sing Auld Lang Syne at the end of the Mayor's Ball and I have recently heard a one man steel band and a Peruvian duet in The Spires shopping precinct. Curry has certainly superseded fish and chips as the nation's most popular dish and Coca Cola has long since taken over from mead.

And now dress. Of course dress that indicates one's occupation is less important now than it used to be as so few people have to wear protective clothing, partly because many dirty jobs are done by robots but probably because more people are just not doing any work.

The young spend much longer at school, college and university; old people, after early retirement, go on living to extreme old age without working and thousands of those ostensibly at work are sitting in motor vehicles doing nothing, unless perhaps they are illegally telephoning base. Where on earth are they all going even if they are moving at all?

Then there are all the accountants, stockbrokers, insurance officials and bank employees. None of them are producing anything, nor are teachers, doctors or carers nor all the people who are shopping till they are dropping, nor the people serving or enjoying the Leisure Industry. So where does the nation's actual material wealth come from? Even the farmers, obviously producers, have to be subsidised.

Women workers love to wear trousers, ponderous shoes and nondescript, unisex hair do's, anything to look unfeminine. Yet if one looks at the long rows of Womens' Magazines in newsagents' shops it is interesting to note that all the front covers, often as many as twenty, depict a pretty, smiling (simpering) young lady's face week after week after week. There's something rather odd about that!

There are not many Men's Magazines but what there are are singularly different.

Before we leave the subject of motoring, it is obvious that the day of the car is over. It has been a wonderful unit in the "forward march of civilisation" but it is taking control of our lives to an extent that few of us realise because it is happening so slowly.

To cope with the estimated increase in the number of cars on our future roads we would have to turn this green and pleasant land into one vast Spaghetti Junction where cars could all circulate to their driver's content without actually arriving anywhere. Clough Williams-Ellis wrote some forty years ago:

> We fling out a brand new by-pass when the first is a chock-full street
> And the glorious day isn't far away when London and Liverpool meet,
> And nothing is left of England where the country used to be
> But a road cut straight, through a building estate,
> And a single specimen *tree.*

Driving recently from Lichfield to Elmdon in the *rush hour!* it came home to me how uncivilised the situation was which impelled hoards of "important" bread winners to travel alone in their luxury five seaters, frustrated by their fellow motorists' stupidity, and the long delays at all of the many roundabouts, coupled with the anticipation of having to hunt for space in a saturated parking lot and arriving late, tired and bad tempered to face their globally important occupations was anything but "civilised living."

On this occasion, I had for many miles been following an immense tanker whose ostentatious slogan told the world that it was carrying "Pure Fresh Spring Water" presumably for consumption by the health conscious individuals for whom tap water is insufficiently immaculate.

I wonder, did the emissions from the diesel engine of the tanker counteract the benefits of the "purer" water on the table?

The day before, I had watched on television a Sudanese housewife walking seven miles to collect indifferent H_2O for her family, an exercise she would repeat when next their needs compelled her to go walkabout *like a queen!*

WAS THIS BETTER?

More of the Buildings

S.M. ON G.

S T. MICHAEL'S on Greenhill has a poetic sounding name and this seems singularly appropriate as it houses the mortal remains of Samuel Johnson's parents and the churchyard contains the bodies of the parents of Philip Larkin.

There is an interesting example of poetic justice as well. The gravestone of the last persons to be hanged in Lichfield has been defaced. Part of the inscription, the word *hanged* has been removed (presumably by a well-wisher) from this memorial to three men who were hanged for *FORGERY.*

It is often said that St. Michael's churchyard is the largest in the country and though I do not think that this has ever been proven, it is certainly very big and has been in use for such a long time that it could very well contain within its perimeter as many dead Lichfield citizens as there are quick ones outside.

Today some of the quick ones go there regularly by car, to exercise their dogs amongst the graves. Just another sign of the times and, after all, gravestones are as convenient as lamp posts any day and you get the best view of the cathedral from St. Michael's green hill.

Following a page about a church with a page about public houses might seem a little improper but we've shown rather a lot of churches and only this little one of a pub and one of a pub sign. Pubs are still more numerous than churches in the city although less so than in the past; there were fifty-six pubs in Lichfield at one time. Now there are only half that number but there are still as many churches as there were in Mediaeval times. The pubs, however tend to have larger congregations.

The best Inn Sign is the George IV, probably because it's a copy of a George Romney portrait.

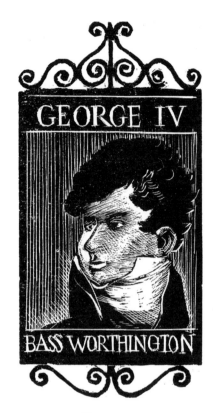

PRINNIE

THE SCALES

NON PEOPLE

ANIMALS and birds of all sorts are quite common in the city. Cats and dogs, of course, but wild creatures as well. Wagtails scuttle about our pavements and supermarket car parks, feral pigeons form a frieze along the roof ridge of St. Mary's church, and grey squirrels and the "magpie mafia" have taken over our gardens, whilst our garden ponds are invaded by that majestic "flying blanket", the grey heron. Even kingfishers can be seen in Beacon Park.

CITY GENT

RENARD

MAFIA

The Close has its pigeons and jackdaws and the two beautiful pools have their numerous seagulls, as well as mallards, coots, the exotic pochard, and other itinerant visitors which now include large flocks (or, when in impressive flight, skeins) of the much maligned Canada geese.

These, rather surprisingly considering their Canadian ancestry, seem to find a frozen pool as puzzling as do our own native species. Luckily, as yet, Stowe Pool has not been invaded by the predatory American crayfish and still has a thriving colony of our own British crustaceans. At dusk you can see bats, foxes and hedgehogs and hear the cry of the occasional owl, and of course there is a lot of rats, but you rarely see or hear them. Neverthless, they are there and do a very good job scavenging the tasty litter left by their human fellow citizens each day, apparently, specifically to sustain their well being.

On Saturday night there are also quite a few drunks.

Of course, nature is not all animal and at the back of some modern houses, on land that was once part of an older and larger garden, can sometimes be found an ancient apple tree; the fruit is never plentiful and certainly does not meet with the size and symmetry requirements of our supermarkets, but it is tasty and good to look at and the tree's gnarled and lichen-covered trunk and branches provide cover for many of our favourite garden birds. They eat the numerous insects that also call it home and, in turn, provide between-meal snacks for our excessive population of cats.

Your average domestic pussy kills more of its fellow creatures (somewhat disagreeably) in a week than does any slavering fox hound in its whole career, so what are we going to do about moggies?

THE KILLER

22

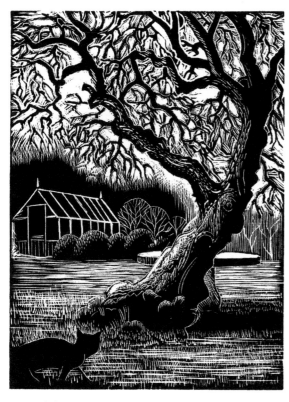

THE LAST OF THE ORCHARD

FELLOW CITIZENS

COLONIALS

23

Our City Fathers

IT seems fitting that our Local Representatives should have a page all to themselves. Our trouble is that we have three lots of councillors, the City, the District and the County, and most local people have great difficulty in understanding which is which, and though they are different councils with very different powers, many of the same people are on the lot. This makes it very difficult for us mere punters to pin them down and very, very easy for them to pass the buck. Hereabouts the buck doesn't seem to stop anywhere.

We elect and re-elect them from time to time and their different hats enable them to pass the wretched buck from council to council until it eventually drops into one of the numerous undiscoverable "Black Holes", where it can quietly disappear.

The picture does not, in fact show a true portrait of any of them, it is just an impression of what councillors seem to be like.

I'm sure the majority of them go into local politics with the very best intentions and most of them are intelligent and well meaning. They work willingly and indeed avidly for smallish rewards, so what goes wrong?

A WELL MEANING GROUP

THE WATERS

LICHFIELD is lucky to have two very fine stretches of water right in the centre of the city, almost dividing it into north and south. Minster Pool, by the cathedral, can still boast a considerable quantity of fine carp as well as a number of fish of lesser dimensions. All sorts of waterfowl feed well on the bread crusts and table scraps thrown to them by our junior citizens and sometimes a kingfisher or a heron quietly diminishes the stock of fish for an early morning meal.

In earlier times the whole area, known as the Moggs, was an impassable swamp until a fine bridge was built on its western border to take the road to Stafford when travellers had got fed up of going all the way round Stowe Pool, our other major lake, just to get to the county town.

Dam Street divides the two pools and gets its name from the dam that at one time controlled the flow of the water that operated the bishop's mill.

Anglers frequent Stowe Pool, indulging in one of mankind's oldest activities, the pursuit of game. They can catch quite a lot (though never when anyone is watching) but I understand that they return all fish back to the water at the end of the day. Tastier fish can be bought nearby.

These sportsmen, who can come from very far afield, are so keen on their chosen *activity* that they often camp out overnight on the pool side to make an early start at dawn on the first day of the coarse fishing season. Most of them seem to smoke!

RISING FISHERMAN

'HAUNTS OF COOT AND HERN'

GOTCHA

STATUES

THERE are many statues round the outside of the cathedral and even though they are mostly kings, saints and angels, not very inspiring. Inside however, there is one outstanding work, the bust of Bishop Wood by Sir Jacob Epstein. More famous is the Sleeping Children by Sir Francis Chantrey but that one is rather too smooth and sentimental for my tastes.

In the town however, we have a beauty, James Boswell, with his back turned towards his great friend Samuel Johnson. These two statues seem to catch the particular spirit of their two subjects. Boswell, a writer whose work and style would go down quite well in a twentieth century tabloid and Johnson, whose profound pontifications are essentially broadsheet. The young girl in marble, plaiting her hair in the library is worth a second glance, but the one which we own but can never see is, probably, the best of the lot. It is of Old Father Time, with scythe and hour glass, dragging along another young girl, to an apparently early grave, or is she perhaps the New Year or even the New Millennium, soon to take over from O.F.T? It is by an Italian, Barcaglia, and is hidden from its owners in the upper floor of the old Art Gallery; you should ask about it!

If Italy asks for it back, as Greece has done in the case of the Elgin Marbles, no doubt we would fight tooth and nail to keep it in the country, and perhaps even look at it now and again.

Then there's Captain Smith in Beacon Park. He piloted the *Titanic* to disaster, and there is a legend, quite untrue, that his statue had been commissioned by Stoke-on-Trent (his home town) but his apparent bad driving caused Stoke to reject it. And so it came to Lichfield, always renowned for its sympathy towards refugees, and now Captain Smith gazes out diligently over Minster Pool where the nearest thing to an iceberg is likely to be a submerged supermarket trolley.

Captain Smith has been much maligned; he was put in charge of an unsinkable ship, and who would have thought that a mere iceberg would have outboxed an unsinkable *anything?*

Lichfield's very nice Art Gallery above the Library, has some good exhibitions, but few citizens know that it's there, and there is also a considerable permanent collection containing several valuable paintings but that's in hiding as well.

We have a lot of "A" boards on our pavements and these can't, or shouldn't, be ignored or you might fall over them! After all, one of them does imply that, "It could be you." On the other hand I think it's best to ignore Charles II outside the cathedral, probably the worst of the lot, and the work of (an active republican) Sir Andrew Wilson, of Sutton Coldfield.

BIOGRAPHER
BOSWELL

IT COULD BE YOU

LICHFIELD'S
"LITTLE MERMAID"

CAPTAIN SMITH

HORTICULTURE

THERE are some beautiful gardens in Lichfield and some expert gardeners, but some of them are special – allotment holders. Allotments are special; they offer one of the few remaining opportunities for uninterrupted self expression. You can grow almost anything as long as it isn't cannabis. Marrows, radishes and parsnips are all O.K. as are sunflowers and forget-me-nots and even dandelions and nettles.

It is possible to make "wine" of varying quality from any of these vegetables. Some of it can be very potent but most of it is horrible. And you are not allowed to grow cannabis, although some allotment holders even now grow their own tobacco.

Over and above all that, you can put up a shed of any shape, as long as it's irregular and in an assortment of materials; corrugated iron, timber, plastic, second hand doors, glass, roofing felt and linoleum. And, until fairly recently, asbestos or a combination of the lot. Planning permission doesn't seem to be necessary.

Water containers can come from established garden centres, breweries, plumbers' yards, or the bathroom that needs rejuvenating. And transport can be anything from an old pram to a Jaguar or, best of all, a beautiful vintage wooden wheelbarrow with an iron tyre shrunk onto a hand-made wooden wheel. An allotment is a wonderful place to get away from it all.

A LITTLE POEM ABOUT ONIONS

Spherical and lovely, chestnut and white,
Layers of bright whiteness and a heart of hot ice,
White roots as anchors and a sun given tan,
Metallic grenade but designed for the pan.

Bronzed and beautiful, copper and green,
Burnished like metal with satin like sheen,
A handful of harvest, straight from the plot,
United with steak and then into the pot.

Part of a group of an artist's still-life.
Together with eggs, a loaf and a knife,
On a tablecloth chequered in primrose and blue,
Then with other ingredients into the stew.

NOT ANOTHER!

THE FLAVOUR OF THE MONTH

TRUG

WORKING ON THE ALLOTMENT

31

City Traditions

LICHFIELD has a lot of most interesting traditional activities which, happily, the council energetically supports, and some of the councillors are never happier than when they are performing as stand up comics at the famous St. George's Court. On Bower Day they all let themselves go. The Bower is a great day out and lots of discerning citizens go out for the day, usually a long way out! But it is much enjoyed by those who like noise and crowds. It is at the beginning of the Bower procession, which perambulates the city streets, that the Mayor enjoys one of the most important activities of his year in office, kissing the Bower Queen.

The procession then proceeds, headed by the Lichfield Morris Men who, dressed in funny costumes, dance all the way round the route, fuelled only by occasional draughts of contaminated water, ie beer! Next comes the Citizen on Horseback who always used to be smoking (traditionally) a large cigar but in these more enlightened days is more likely, like the rest of Lichfield, to be observed chewing gum (as can be seen from the city's pavements).

The Sheriff's Ride is another spectacular occasion, with up to a hundred mounted participants, a splendid sight. They are led by the current sheriff who is nearly always a councillor these days, (ever since an earlier council started financing the event instead of expecting the incumbent to pay for the honour out of his own pocket). Mr Jorrocks said that a fox hunt was "the image of war without its guilt." Could our Sheriff's Ride be described as "the image of fox hunting without its guilt"?

Long may it continue, and through proper countryside and not suburbia!

Then there is the Court of Arraye, the Mayoral Court of the Worshipful Company of Smiths, the Johnson Celebrations, and more recently the Pancake Race, and the Darwin Walk around the city's (still fairly) green necklace.

Of course, the cathedral and the churches put on regular colourful events, Christmas is usually the best but Easter and Ascension day come close after, and from time to time the army puts on a showy parade, colours flying, drums beating and bayonets fixed! There is some sort of honour attached to this ceremony, but I can never remember whether it goes to the troops for putting it on or to the city for putting up with it!

CITIZEN ON HORSEBACK

LICHFIELD MORRIS MEN

THE SHERIFF'S RIDE

Now, the most important event of the year must be the International Festival of the Arts which is based at the cathedral and which some people say is elitist. The organisers would dispute this most emphatically but when some of the tickets cost £35.00, some would-be punters are undoubtedly discouraged. *Only £35.00* as most present day advertisements would put it. Have you noticed that now *Only* nearly always precedes the pound sign be it advertising motor cars, television sets or Chinese takeaways, and *Only* is usually preceded by *From*?

Nevertheless we do have some other new and relatively cheap festivals. The Jazz Festival is one and the Folk Festival provides the opportunity to watch Morris and Clog dancing and the like at no cost at all. It will be well worth supporting when they include the Can Can!

Then of course there's the Fringe which used to operate from the old Arts Centre (a grade II *twisted* building), but since that home has been condemned the Fringe is not what it was.

There is however, another Fringe to the Fringe, centred at St. Chad's church and I have performed there personally. I've recited from the pulpit – some of my own verse at that! And now I *know* why people aspire to the priesthood. The upturned, expectant faces of the public, as seen from the pulpit, in the splendid Gothic surroundings warms the cockles of one's heart. I'm just astonished that there isn't a surplice (collective noun) of clergymen in every parish.

Then there's the Pancake Race, hardly the Grand National but quite entertaining and involving some good-looking fillies. It coincides with the Shrovetide Fair, a mini Bower where you can see the Mayor driving a Dodgem car, in full regalia, and it's easy to see on that occasion why our councillors are sometimes led astray.

The Lichfield Mysteries is becoming a re-established tradition and the Players and the Operatic Society are well established regulars and I am sure there are many others.

Of course, most of these events have a disastrous effect on the free flow of traffic through the town, but long may they continue!

ONE BIG FIDDLE

THE DARWIN WALK

EVENING SHADOWS

YOUNG PEOPLE

IT is often said that our young citizens are not interested in joining local organisations, not the Civic Society, nor the Society of Artists and certainly not the W.I. or T.W.G., but it's like that where ever you go. If they have got a job, they have to work hard to keep it and if they haven't got a job they feel uncomfortable amongst those in work. Those with money to spend do, however, do their own thing. They play badminton and squash, they go jogging and swimming and quite a lot of our pubs have active football teams. It is indeed quite inspiring to see the players assembling outside their local before their Sunday morning encounter with a neighbouring outfit.

Lots of Keep Fitters (turn of the century equivalent of Do Gooders?) drive quite a long way to the Sports Centres, play a vigorous game, have a snack and a drink and then drive home. If they'd just walked both ways and cut out the calorie intake they'd have done themselves just as much good and would not have contributed to asthma-inducing pollution.

It's much the same with driving the kids to school, protecting them from the dangers of too many motor cars; and of course, when those kids get to school, they are subjected to Compulsory Games. Many of them become couch potatoes, turned off by the very compulsory "games" that are supposed to be so good for them. Compulsory anything is a bit off-putting but compulsory "games" sounds a contradiction in terms. They decide on leaving school that Kipling's "Muddied oafs and flannelled fools" are all right on telly but too much energy is required actually to get involved.

Then there are the Ravers who would disdain to associate with anyone over the age of thirty and wouldn't be seen dead at the Mayor's Ball, but become ecstatically submerged in the noisy rhythm and flashing lights of their *night spot* gathering ground, where they enjoy swinging and twisting, chewing and smoking, sweating and groping until the small hours and final chucking out time. All part of the Lichfield scene!

RAVERS

COMPULSORY GAMES

THE PARKS

CAR parks, if you include the multi-storey ones, cover a greater acreage of Lichfield's open space than anything else, except, of course the pools which would have cost too much to convert. But we are very lucky in having in Beacon Park, a beautiful rural landscape coming right into the heart of the city.

There are some other good parks as well; the Friary gardens, also within the city boundaries, are a continual joy and a credit to the spenders of our taxes, and the Darwin Walk is a peri-urban park almost unique to Lichfield. More than that, some of our schools, even the inner city ones have playing fields matching up to those in many public schools, but Beacon Park is the jewel in the crown and we are at least allowed to go into it.

Linked with Minster Pool, Stowe Pool and the cycle track/footpath which runs through the open land behind St. Chad's church, it enshrines a rural pathway that connects the open countryside on the west of the city to the open countryside on the east, another very special feature.

Beacon Park was left to the city by landowner Colonel Swinfen Broun in 1948 and, from being the pleasure grounds of a very few of what was then called "the Quality", it became the pleasure grounds of the many who aspired to a description no more elevated than "us".

So we demolished the fine, if dilapidated, gentleman's residence and put up a number of sheds (quite possibly funded by the famous Conduit Lands Trust) and the splendid horseflesh of days gone by has given way to seesaws and swings and other instruments of fun. A golf course has absorbed about half the estate and the elegant attire of the landed gentry has been replaced by the carefully considered casual scruffiness which is now the height of fashion. And of course, the landed gentry can still go in!

SWINGS AND KNOCKABOUTS

Nevertheless, I wouldn't wish all the local stately homes to become public property. Some of the fairly stately ones are in good hands and help to preserve traditional values that can be appreciated by us all, even at a distance. Also, they don't get turned into car parks. There was once a very popular bandstand in Beacon Park but it has been removed, apparently because people now prefer listening to their own canned music in solitude. Now you *have* to take your own canned music and listen in solitude. There are, however, many old Lichfeldians who would dearly love to see the bandstand re-established so that they can enjoy live entertainment in the fresh air, in the company of their friends.

IN THE PARK

This last picture is of a water pump in the Close. It's been there for two hundred years, for the particular use of the residents, and is a very solid stone example of the architecture of the day. The pump handle has gone but through the slot where it was located can be seen the mechanical paraphernalia that once operated the system.

It is interesting to compare the confidence the residents felt in their plumbers (it would have needed a team of stone masons to dismantle enough of it to change a washer) and the confidence they had in their neighbours' honesty, for there can still be seen the metal staple that once held the chain that attached the metal cup, or, since it was the Close, goblet, to the stonework — but that appears to have been *nicked*.